Giacomo Summa

Social TV

Giacomo Summa

Social TV

The Future of Television in the Internet Age

LAP LAMBERT Academic Publishing

Impressum/Imprint (nur für Deutschland/only for Germany)
Bibliografische Information der Deutschen Nationalbibliothek: Die Deutsche Nationalbibliothek verzeichnet diese Publikation in der Deutschen Nationalbibliografie; detaillierte bibliografische Daten sind im Internet über http://dnb.d-nb.de abrufbar.

Coverbild: www.ingimage.com

Verlag: LAP LAMBERT Academic Publishing GmbH & Co. KG
Heinrich-Böcking-Str. 6-8, 66121 Saarbrücken, Deutschland
Telefon +49 681 3720-310, Telefax +49 681 3720-3109
Email: info@lap-publishing.com

Herstellung in Deutschland:
Schaltungsdienst Lange o.H.G., Berlin
Books on Demand GmbH, Norderstedt
Reha GmbH, Saarbrücken
Amazon Distribution GmbH, Leipzig
ISBN: 978-3-8473-3957-1

Imprint (only for USA, GB)
Bibliographic information published by the Deutsche Nationalbibliothek: The Deutsche Nationalbibliothek lists this publication in the Deutsche Nationalbibliografie; detailed bibliographic data are available in the Internet at http://dnb.d-nb.de.

Cover image: www.ingimage.com

Publisher: LAP LAMBERT Academic Publishing GmbH & Co. KG
Heinrich-Böcking-Str. 6-8, 66121 Saarbrücken, Germany
Phone +49 681 3720-310, Fax +49 681 3720-3109
Email: info@lap-publishing.com

Printed in the U.S.A.
Printed in the U.K. by (see last page)
ISBN: 978-3-8473-3957-1

Social TV: the Future of Television in the Internet Age
By

Giacomo Summa

Submitted to the MIT Sloan School of Management on May 6, 2011
in partial fulfillment of the requirements for the degree of Master
of Science in Management Studies

ABSTRACT

Television's influence on culture and society has been widely acknowledged for many years.
On the other hand, with the diffusion of the web and of social networks such as Facebook and
Twitter, used in concert with television, the TV experience has become much more interactive and it
is now impossible not to acknowledge that television has also become a driving force for social
interaction. Furthermore, the parallel diffusion of internet videos and user generated content,
fostered by YouTube in particular, has provided the population with a different approach to media
and television in particular: consumers have also become producers.
This work analyzes how the different technological improvements have changed the definition of
television. Special attention is given to how Facebook and Twitter have influenced some of TV's
fundamental properties such as liveness, character-centric storylines and flow and to what the
YouTube phenomena means for television.
The thesis concludes with a forecast about television's future, which confirms the main argument of
this thesis: television is increasingly social.

Thesis Supervisor: Michael Cusumano
Title: SMR Distinguished Professor of Management

Index

1. Introduction

Assuming the truth of Aristotle's famous saying, "man is by nature a social animal", it is no surprise that television, which makes up for a large amount of our daily life (according to Nielsen, Americans over 2 years of age spent an average of 154 hours and 4 minutes per month watching TV in Q4 2010), has tremendous consequences on society and the way society thinks and interacts.

Television's success dates way back in time. Television's first hit in the U.S. was Texaco Star Theater (telecast from 1948 to 1956) starring Milton Berle (aka Mr. Television). The show was so successful that, according to Rose (2011), Detroit's reservoir levels dropped every Tuesday night at 9.00 pm because most people didn't go to the toilet during the whole time of the show (page 5). However, what is perhaps one of the first and most remembered events that proved television's role in shaping society and political opinion was the first televised presidential debate between John Fitzgerald Kennedy and Richard Nixon, which was watched by an estimated 70 million viewers. Several scholars argued that it was Kennedy's tanned appearance and confidence that gave him a boost in popularity, secured him the lead in the polls and ultimately made him win the elections over Nixon, who appeared tired and pale instead.

Television has traditionally offered common material for conversation and has served the function of "window to the world" for a fairly sedentary public. An excellent example of this is the broadcast of the landing on the moon on the 20th of July 1969. The Apollo 11's mission was watched by millions of people all over the world and has marked the lives of entire generations, especially the younger ones, who followed the events through extensive television coverage.

The power of television has been recognized outside of the US as well. Italian Prime Minister Silvio Berlusconi, whose media empire is considered the main source of his political power, famously said: "don't you understand, that if something is not on television it doesn't exist!". It is no mystery that television can shape and eventually skew people's perception of reality. If television equals reality, then controlling television can be a very powerful instrument to define people's perspectives on the world. But the truth is that television's power over society and politics has often been more subtle than a direct manipulation of reality. For example, television shows and personalities have had an immense role in defining popular culture, which has in turn influenced people's perceptions and politics.

1.1. TV as a Social Medium

While television's influence on culture and society is widely acknowledged, not all media scholars have agreed on TV being a social medium, a medium for or to facilitate social interaction. For example, in an early study on television, Rudolph Arnheim (1935) questioned how social TV really was going to be: "television will make up for actual physical presence even more than does radio. All the more isolated will be the individual in his retreat, and the balance of trade will be correspondingly precarious: an enormous influx of riches, consumption without services in return. The pathetic hermit, squatting in his room, hundreds of miles away from the scene that he experiences as his present life, the 'viewer' who cannot even laugh or applaud without feeling ridiculous, is the final product of a century-long development, which has led from the campfire, the market place, and the arena to the lonesome consumer of spectacles today." Later on Raymond Williams (1974), in his classic book "Television", acknowledged how "within the broadcasting model there was this deep contradiction, of centralized transmission and privatized reception" (page 24).

6

While some might share some of the arguments of Arnheim's concerned forecast or Williams' analysis, it is now impossible not to acknowledge the potential that Television has not only as a mere influence on society, but also as a driving force for social interaction. *As pointed out by Harboe, Massey, Metcalf, Wheatley and Romano (2008),* while the stereotype presents television as an asocial activity, TV has historically provided topics for conversations, eased interaction and promoted feelings of togetherness (page 1). Later in the thesis, I will provide examples (personal and not) of how television can become an important aspect of our social life, with fictional characters or complicated storylines becoming the common subject of our thoughts and of our discussions.

While it is useful to reason about television and its social aspects since its inception, TV's social component has certainly become an even more concrete reality in the recent years. Several different technologies have influenced the way people consume television, but it is the World Wide Web "revolution" that further extended the social potential of television and the concept of TV as a medium that fosters social interaction. This happened in particular with the introduction of social networks such as Facebook and Twitter, quickly assuming the function of "digital water coolers", and platform such as YouTube, which revolutionized the way the content is created and distributed.

Some scholars have found appropriate to use the term "social TV" to describe the current trends in the television business: as Klim and Monpetit (2008) wrote, "while the social aspect of TV is not new in and of itself, the term, social TV, has emerged fairly recently to describe a new breed of video services that integrate other communication services like voice, chat, context awareness, and peer ratings to support a shared TV experience with one's peer groups"

(Page 4). While this seems to almost define an entity, social TV, separated from TV itself, more accurately it defines a shift to a definition of TV that takes into account the convergence of media, in particular internet and television. As television and web converge, social networks become an integrating part of the television experience, impossible to be detached from the medium TV.

1.2. Thesis' Structure, Objectives and Methodology

This thesis principally aims at analyzing the impact that the internet is having on television by increasing its social potential. I will show how the internet and social media might be what is ultimately saving television by re-imposing liveness, long-lost to DVR devices, by facilitating character-centric storylines and by re-inventing flow, all very important components of the television experience. In fact, ultimately television can only survive if it is social. Fortunately it appears that the TV business is slowly adapting itself to accept what sociality means in the internet era: for example, it means loss of control for the producers and increased power for the spectators and it means producing engaging shows which foster conversation.

From this thesis it will become apparent that at this early stage of integration between internet and TV, there are still a lot of opportunities to be exploited. I believe that in the next few years, successful understanding and implementation of the trends discussed in this work will bring new revenue streams both to the content producers and to a series of newly-born companies, which are working very hard to make television always more social and interactive.

My hope is that this work can help the reader understand the current state of television, while offering insights on what path the TV business should follow in order to survive the current struggles it is experiencing.

This thesis is mainly a review and an analysis of existing literature on the topic of television. Literature used spans from television-theory classics such as Raymond Williams' "Television", written in 1974, to very recent articles from major newspapers and popular social media blogs such as Mashable and TechCrunch. Throughout the thesis, I also offer a brief exposition of what established companies and startups are doing to try to conquer the newly born sector of "social television".

In chapter two, "From the Network Era to Television Today", I will go through the different phases of television's history, from the so-called network era to the present state of television. The knowledge of television's different eras is fundamental to understand many of the practices that are still typical of today's television business.

In the current process of TV transformation, some of what have been historically considered the most significant properties of television, such as liveness, character-centric storylines and flow have been re-defined, perhaps accentuated, and in certain cases rediscovered thanks to social networks such as Facebook and Twitter. I will analyze this trend in chapter three, "The Effect of Social Networks on Television".

Furthermore, I will explain how television's historical tendency to impose its content on the audience, together with its association with the "black box" we have traditionally used to watch TV, has become obsolete thanks to websites such as YouTube. This topic will be covered in chapter four, "YouTube and Internet videos".

Finally I dedicated chapter five to what the future of television might look like according to several experts interviewed by CISCO Systems.

2. From the Network Era to Television Today

U.S. Television, but there are strong similarities in other developed countries, has gone through different eras, which differed for their industrial practices, amongst other things. In particular, Amanda Lotz (2007) distinguishes between three different periods in television history: first, the "network era", which went from 1952 circa through the mid-1980s. Then a so-called "multi-channel" transition and finally what she defines as the "post-network" era (page 7). The main characteristics of the different eras are also exposed in the table at page 10.

The "network era" is so important in the history of television that, in spite of all the changes of the past twenty-five years, the norms which developed in this period still strongly influence the practices of today's television business. The network era in the U.S belonged, as the name would suggest, to NBC, CBS and ABC, which were first established in Radio. The network era is characterized by limited program choice and mass audiences, a factor that allowed the networks to assume a very important role in defining post-war American identity.

Just as in radio, the traditional business model for early television relied on a single sponsor for each program. This model was eliminated partially as a consequence of the quiz show scandals of the late 1950s and early 1960s, which exposed advertisers' readiness to mislead the public by favoring certain contestants in the name of more entertaining programs. It was at this point that TV switched to the "magazine-like" advertising, with several advertisers who paid for 30 seconds commercials to be inserted at regular intervals within the TV shows. Companies bought their advertising space based on networks guarantees of reaching and addressing a certain audience, despite the lack of proper methods for calculating this audience. It follows that that the network-era saw disproportionate power in the hands of the networks, which could impose their content on viewers, while forcing their conditions on advertisers.

During the "multi-channel" transition television went through lots of changes, but these were slow and gradual enough that allowed the television industry to operate pretty much under the same norms as it did in the network era. New technologies such as the videocassette recorder (VCR), the remote control and analogue cable system empowered the viewers and gave them more extended choices and control. NBC, CBS and ABC's leadership was challenged both by new broadcasting networks (FOX - launched in 1986, The WB – launched in 1995 and UPN – launched in 1995) and by subscription cable channels, which introduced a business model based mainly on monthly subscription fees instead of advertising. The viewers experience was principally changed as a consequence of the increased choice in the content they could consume. As a result, during the 1980s the audience share of broadcast networks decreased from 90 to 64 %, losing ground to cable channels (Lotz, page 13). Despite the introduction of the new broadcast networks, this percentage further decreased to 58 % by the end of the 1999/2000 season , and down to 46% at the end of the 2004/2005 season. By 2004, 85 % of households had subscribed to "alternative distribution systems" such as cable and satellite and the average home was receiving 100 channels.

As Lotz notes, "the explosion of content providers throughout the multichannel transition enabled viewers to increasingly isolate themselves in enclaves of specific interests"(page 14). As a consequence of this multi-channel transition, both broadcast networks and cable channels started developing programming that could satisfy precise audience members as opposed to try to produce shows which would be "least objectionable to the entire family" (page 14). Producers were able to target always more narrow audiences: for example, channels specifically for women were created. Cable channels' ability to better target audiences made them a very satisfying option for viewers, when compared to more generalist broadcasting channels. At the same time, advertisers were also very much interested in these very targeted channels because they could be better aware of what type of customer they were reaching, augmenting the potential of their ads. On the other hand, broadcasting channels' larger audiences allow them to obtain larger revenues from advertisers, making them usually less constraint in their budgeting choices and better able to develop new expensive programs.

Finally, according to Lotz (2007), what distinguishes our current "post-network era", which began approximately in the mid-2000s, from the multi-channel transition is that the changes in television have been so extensive that it became impossible for the industry to fully preserve the same old practices typical of the network era. On the other hand, "post-network" shouldn't suggest that networks have completely lost their relevance, but that their power over viewers is substantially decreasing, as we shall see in the rest of this thesis. In particular, as Lotz (2007) writes, the post network era allows viewers "to choose among programs produced in any decade, by amateurs and professionals, and to watch this programming on demand and for viewing on main "living room" sets, computer screens, or portable devices" (page 19).

Production Component	Network Era	Multi-Channel Transition	Post-Network Era
Technology	Television	VCR remote control Analog cable	DVR, VOD Portable devices (iPod, PSP) Mobile Phones Slingbox Digital Cable
Creation	Deficit Financing	Fin-syn rules, surge of independents, end of fin-syn conglomeration and co-production	Multiple financing norms, variation in cost structure and aftermarket value; opportunities for amateur production
Distribution	Bottleneck, definite windows, exclusivity	Cable increase possible outlets	Erosion of time between windows, and exclusivity; content anytime, anywhere
Advertising	:30 ads, upfront market	Subscription, experimentation with alternatives to :30 ads	Co-existence of multiple models - :30, placement, integration, branded entertainment, sponsorship; multiple user supported-transactional and subscription
Audience Measurement	Audimeters, diaries sampling	People Meters, sampling	Portable Poeple Meters, census measure

Characteristics of Production Components in Each Period

Source: The Television will be revolutionized. Amanda D. Lotz. Page 8

A very important fact that has strongly influenced at least the first part of the post-network era has been the wide diffusion of the Digital Video Recorder (DVR), which was first introduced in 1999, and is a technology that allows people to easily program the recording of TV shows in order to watch them when most convenient. A similar technology, the Videocassette Recorder (VCR), was popularized during the multichannel transition. However, since the VCR was much more complicated to use than the DVR, it was never broadly used as a time-shifting technology, but ultimately only as an alternative source of revenues for the film and TV industry, which found an alternative distribution system in the market for videocassettes. On the other hand, the DVR was broadly adopted to fulfill the function that it was intended for. This changed extensively the perception the public had of television. For example, Lotz (2007) reports a study from Jason Mittell in which he explains that when his child asks "what is on television?", she is really asking what shows are stored on the hard drive and not what is currently on live TV (page 18). While time-shifting could per se be harmless for the television business, viewers' possibility of skipping the commercials, historically television's source of income, has been seen as a major threat by TV executives, who worked on developing alternative forms of advertisement, such as product placement and brand integration, to satisfy their clients' needs. What is certainly clear is that future business models for the TV business will have to go beyond the 30-seconds advertisements that have characterized most of television's history.

2.1. The Internet and the Survival of Television

Television's transformation during the past few years has been so fundamental that some speculated that television was a dead medium, culturally irrelevant in the new society prospected by the more open and collaborative internet era. Already in the 1990s, Bruce Sterling (1995), a science fiction author and creator of the Dead Media Project, wrote that "the centralized, dinosaurian one-to-many media that roared and trampled through the twentieth century are poorly adapted to the postmodern technological environment". Furthermore, younger viewers have gotten accustomed to expect more from television. Henry Jenkins (2006) calls young viewers "Media-actives", people who are used to cable television, TiVo and the internet and who take a much more active role in their media consumption (page 244).

In spite of this, television's death forecast should be considered at least premature. As Jenkins (2006) notes, "history teaches us that old media never die – and they don't even necessarily fade away. What dies are simply the tools we use to access media content – the 8-track, the Beta tape" (page 13). So the black box, the "delivery technology" that most people are accustomed to call TV, might become old-fashioned and get replaced. But not the medium television itself, which evolves instead.

Surprisingly, what is keeping television alive, the focus of this thesis, is what many perceived as its biggest threat: the internet. Strangelove (2010) reports that Nielsen company concluded that Americans have never watched more television, but that television viewing is increasingly shifting to the internet (page 169). On top of offering a new platform for video distribution, the web revolution introduced social networks such as Facebook and Twitter, which are enhancing the television experience of today's viewers, allowing for more interaction and for more active participation. In this process, television's definition is changing extensively.

In the following chapters, I will explain first how the definition of television is changing because of social networks, Twitter and Facebook in particular, and then how internet videos and YouTube in particular are also contributing to this changing definition.

3. The Effect of Social Networks on Television

Facebook's more than 600 million and Twitter's almost 200 million users are a strong indication that these web tools are part of people's lives and are changing the way people interact. Along with their success, the television experience has been transformed, and with it the way it influences the population and it allows for social interaction.

The use that has been done of social networks such as Twitter and Facebook in concert with TV viewing, principally as forums to discuss TV shows, had The Economist (2010) liken the two websites to "digital water coolers". People want to extend their couch beyond their home in the hope of sharing their TV watching experience with as many people (whether friends or strangers) as possible, even if only virtually. As Klym and Montpetit (2008) wrote, "a person's social networks are replacing the typical family room of the 1950s. These virtual communities can extend far beyond the home to span entire neighborhoods, cities, countries, and hemispheres" (page 5). Therefore, if television already facilitated social interaction in the past, nowadays this property has been certainly further emphasized. According to Poniewozik (2010) " contrary to its image, TV is also inherently social [...] People throw parties around it; they watch it to be able to talk to other people about it. Social media enhance rather than replace events like the Oscars and — important when DVRs let people record shows and skip the ads — make watching them in real time worthwhile so people can be in on the conversation. Because as much as we like to watch, we like to talk."

As social networks are strongly contributing in redefining the television experience, I will now go through some of what major media scholars have considered the main properties of television and discuss how they have been

17

influenced by social networks. A particular attention will be given to how social media are contributing to changing or even rediscovering some of the properties that are traditionally associated to television, such as liveness, character-centric storylines and flow.

3.1. Liveness

Liveness has been traditionally understood as a feature of the medium television and it has been perceived as a key differentiator of Television from other media such as cinema and print. For example Herbert Zettl, quoted by Feuer (1983), tried to define some of the ontological differences between television and cinema (always interpreted as a "sister" medium): "while the film frame is a concrete record of the past, the television frame (when live) is a reflection of the living, constantly changing present". Furthermore, "while film can reflect upon our world or pretend to be current, it is totally deterministic; the end of the story is fixed as soon as the reel is put on the projector. Live television, on the other hand, lives off the instantaneousness and uncertainty of the moment very much like we do in actual life" (page 13). While Jane Feuer (1983) rejects the notion of identity between liveness and reality, she agrees with the fact that television is ontologically a live medium. Referencing Heath and Skirrow, she writes that "by postulating an equivalence between time of event, time of television creation and transmission-viewing time, television as an institution identifies all messages emanating from the apparatus as "live"" (p.14). Liveness is perceived in the ability to transmit an event as it occurs. In this sense, even pre-recorded events can be intended as live since the event itself is the transmission. It follows that liveness can be deterministic, in the case of pre-scripted shows transmitted live or non-deterministic, in case for example of sport broadcasts.

But a lot has changed since Feuer and Zettl have published their studies. The liveness nowadays does not reside anymore in the simple transmission, but in the actual conversing on social networks at the time of transmission. Two trends have concurred to this redefinition of liveness. The first relevant trend,

19

indicating a threat to liveness, is the increasing diffusion of "time-shifting" technologies such as TiVo, which allow viewers to watch their favorite shows whenever they want to. According to a poll conducted for Comcast and reported by AP (2010), sixty percent of American own a DVR device. The second trend is reported by Deloitte (2011), which found that of 2,000 American consumers ages 14 to 75, 42 percent sometimes surfed the Web while watching TV, and 26 percent sometimes sent instant messages or texts. This tendency is likely to become even more common as smartphones and tablets become more widespread.

Both trends are summarized by Rose (2011): "Americans are watching more TV than ever - but, like their counterparts around the globe, increasingly they do it on their own schedule, and at the same time they're uploading their own videos on YouTube, posting their snapshots on Flickr, sharing their thoughts on Blogger or WordPress, and connecting with one another through MySpace and Facebook" (page 86-87). As previously mentioned, the first trend (time-shifting), which began in 1999 with the introduction of ReplayTV and TiVo, has upset advertisers, whose ads get often skipped through. The second trend (the contemporaneous consumption of TV and internet), more recent, is having the opposite effect and it might help TV networks regain as many viewers right when the show airs. Since TV revenues come, as reported by the International Television Expert Group (2010) at a rate of 45 to 50 % from TV advertising, 40 to 45% from subscription fees and 10% circa from public funding, it is no surprise that TV executives worry about DVR technologies. On the other hand, TV executives are demonstrating to be much more enthusiastic about social networks, Twitter in particular.

3.1.1. Liveness and Social Networks

A data is particularly interesting: Twitter's trending topics, the most tweeted-about topics on Twitter in any particular moment, are very often related to entertainment, making up for 28 % of the trending topics in 2010 according to a study by "What the trend" reported by Mashable (2010). Twitter is where TV-related conversations seem to be concentrated on the web. The social network is increasingly becoming an instrument to re-impose liveness on the audience.

Indeed, the use of Social Networks, mainly Twitter, while watching TV is credited with making the 2011 Grammy Awards the highest rated in a decade. As reported by Silverman (2011), the Grammy Awards were the top Twitter Trend in the week between the 11 and the 17 of February. Artists such as Justin Bieber and Lady Gaga, who have millions of Twitter fans, were discussed during the show, whether with congratulatory remarks, insults or other comments. Friends' tweets, hilarious tweets or simply the quantity of tweets in turn attracted others who were not watching the show, but wanted to "join the conversation".

Tsotsis (2011 - TechCrunch) reports that on the 2011 Oscars, over 20 Oscar-related terms were tracked on Twitter and the outcome was a total of 1,269,970 tweets, 1,663,458,778 potential impressions and 388,717 users tweeting during the show's live broadcast. The most re-tweeted tweet was from @TheOnion receiving 2963 tweets: "How rude — not a single character from Toy Story 3 bothered to show up. #oscars". 2011 Oscar's co-host, James Franco was tweeting during the live-broadcast of the Oscars, giving behind-the-scene information about what was happening, adding an extra layer to the show for the audience. He sent several pictures from the backstage, while with other stars or by himself, preparing to go on stage. Because of this, he was the second most mentioned account (after The Academy's account, @TheAcademy), with 6627 mentions during the show. But Franco had joined Twitter just few days prior to the Oscars and he didn't have the same social media power that music stars like Lady Gaga (Twitter's most followed account with over 9 million followers) or Justin Bieber (with more than 8 million followers) have. This is perhaps one reason for which the Oscars were not as much as a success as, for example, the 2011 Grammy Awards, which were the most watched in a decade. Indeed, Tsotsis (2011) comments that the spike of 12,000 tweets per minute is nothing in comparison with the 17,000 tweets in a single minute seen during the Super Bowl and The Grammy. It follows that part of the effort that TV producers will have to make in the recent future will be directed towards attracting the best stars and most connected people to tweet during the various live events.

If well implemented, this process has the immediate consequence of turning away people from their DVR devices because users do not want to miss out on the live conversation. It must be said that events such as the Grammy and the Oscars or such as news reports and sports events, have traditionally already been perceived as events whose value relies in watching them as they happen. So what is perhaps an even more interesting effect of social networks on television is that they offer a sense of liveness to pre-recorded events: to be up to date on the conversation, one has to watch *Mad Men, How I Met Your Mother* or whatever show one loves, as soon as it is aired. Not only watching the show live makes the experience more entertaining (while also avoiding spoilers), but tweeting and reading online comments about what's happening in the episode becomes an integrating part of the show. Chloe Sladden, head of media partnerships at Twitter, interviewed by Fast Company (2011) describes the influence of Twitter on TV: "What we're seeing now is that Twitter is, in fact, about flocking audiences back to a shared experience, and that usually means a live one". Sladden adds that "if you're not watching live -- and reading the comments from friends, your favorite celebrities, and even total strangers via Twitter -- you're missing half the show".

Using "Google Realtime", I was able to look at the users' behavior on Twitter for a live broadcast of a new episode of How I Met Your Mother aired on the 21st of March on CBS. There was a spike in references to "How I met Your Mother" as the show began at 8pm eastern time. Several people were indeed "checking-into" the show in social networks such as gomiso.com and getglue.com, which allow people to share what they are watching and automatically post a message such as "I'm watching X" on Twitter and Facebook, further facilitating the starting of a conversation. The episode I watched had one of the main characters of the show, Barney, finally meeting his dad, who is played by John Lithgow, an actor who is remembered by many for playing the role of a cruel serial killer on Showtime's Dexter. Many comments reflected on this and wondered whether they were the only ones to feel uncomfortable with a serial killer playing Barney's dad. Within seconds, viewers' inquiries were satisfied as several similar comments started to flow through Twitter in reply to the initial comments. After not too long, part of the public had concluded that Barney's dad hadn't been with his son for the past 30 years because he was killing people instead. At 8.30, when the show ended, the number of tweets started decreasing, but the discussion kept on for a while. People felt their thoughts were legitimized when they ascertained that they were not alone in thinking in a certain way.

Liveness can perhaps be intended as a compromise to satisfy television's need for sociality, both for producers and for viewers: viewers want to share their experience with their friends and with as many people as possible, as public discussions on Twitter prove. Sometimes it is only liveness that allows for the conversation to exist at all: watching a TV show in one's own schedule has the downside that very few people, if any, are sharing the same experience. At the same time, TV executives want the highest possible number of people to watch their content and the commercials proposed during the breaks. Liveness allow for the television experience to be shared by the highest possible quantity of people and as David Reed of the MIT Media Lab notes, "from a business point of view, almost all of the value (economic utility) of our communications arises out of the shared context that we have created" (Klim and Montpetit, page 7).

But Twitter's blessing by TV companies goes beyond the incentive they have in having increased audiences for their commercials. As Craig Engler (2010), senior vice president of Syfy digital, explains in an article about the 10 reasons every TV exec needs to start tweeting, "I can tell if that joke we all worried about in the new episode was funny or not, if a complicated storyline made sense, etc. It's an endless stream of feedback that you can dip in and out of".

Some producers have learnt the importance to use social networks to "immerse" their audiences in the TV show experience, while increasing viewership thanks to further public's engagement. Certain TV shows are indeed quickly mastering the art of starting the conversation on Twitter and Facebook. For example they are partnering with entertainment check-in websites such as gomiso.com and getglue.com to offer special badges (given as a reward on the website) to people checking into their shows while it is broadcasted. These websites (which are also easy-to-use iPhone apps) foster the start of the conversation by creating momentum around a TV show, as described above for

How I Met Your Mother. A proof of the interest that networks and entertainment companies have towards this type of Social TV apps is the recent acquisition by Yahoo of 12 weeks-old company IntoNow for an undisclosed sum between 20 and 30 million dollars. IntoNow is able to recognize what one is watching on TV (fundamentally it is the "Shazam" of television) and it then notifies the user when someone from his own social networks is watching the same show.

In other instances, such as for the hit TV-show Glee, the most tweeted-about TV show, FOX has asked cast and producers to tweet during the live broadcast of a rerun of the pilot of the show. While these initiatives have been usually very much appreciated by the audience, we shall see in the case of *Mad Men* exposed below that it is not always possible to start, shape and control the public's conversation.

3.2. Characters and Narration in the Social Networks Era

Narrative has an important place in the definition of television. According to Rose (2011), "every new medium has given rise to a new form of narrative" (page 2). As Marie-Laure Ryan (2006) explains, "the type of narrative that takes full advantage of the idiosyncrasies of the TV medium is not the self-contained Aristotelian plot but the never-ending serial with multiple characters, parallel plot lines, and largely episodic structure". Ryan further reasons that this type of narrative puts more focus to the characters than to the action(page 60).

I must confess that when the post "Donald Draper, you are a jerk!!!" appeared on my Facebook newsfeed, I couldn't help but reply. As I found myself writing a well thought of email to a long lost friend with the only purpose of objecting to some frivolous comment she had made about *Mad Men*, one of my favorite TV shows, I was forced to acknowledge how deeply can a TV show, together with its characters, affect one's life. Television's social component also derives from the fact that it provides characters whom viewers can identify themselves with or whom they can care about. Indeed, one of the reasons why I like a show such as *Mad Men* so much is perhaps because sometimes I cannot avoid to empathize with Donald Draper's character, no matter how much of a "jerk" he is.

It was always the case that the TV narration, compared to that of movies, was much more flexible in the way the story was defined and had more room for viewers to shape the story. As Ryan (2006) argues, "because TV narration stretches out indefinitely in time, its plot is continually in the process of being written, which means that the audience can offer feedback to the scriptwriters, either indirectly through polls or directly through such institutions as fan clubs, fan magazines, and online chat groups. This feature makes the TV serial narrative far more interactive than movie drama" (page 61).

But if TV shows' plot was fairly open in the past, it is much more open now that both web and social media allow viewers to interact with their favorite shows almost instantaneously and without having to make almost any effort. But together with TV allowing for more sociality and interaction, show creators are partially losing control of their stories as viewers use social networks to modify or rewrite the stories in their own ways. In his Book, "The art of immersion" (2011), Frank Rose narrates about how a group of fans of the show *Man Men*, a drama series about a group of advertisers in the 1960s aired on cable TV channel AMC, started tweeting as their favorite fictional characters without consulting with the show creators and producers. According to Rose's account, Paul Isakson, himself an advertiser from Mineapolis, started tweeting as Don Draper, *Mad Men*'s main character, in August 2008, not long after the beginning of the second season of the show, and was shortly followed by other online users who started tweeting as others of the show's characters (page 78). Isakson's first tweet as Don Draper was: "drinking a scotch with Roger so he doesn't feel like an alcoholic" - where Roger stands for Roger Sterling, Draper's fellow partner at the Sterling Cooper advertising agency. Peggy Olson, *Mad Men*'s first female copyrighter also started tweeting, either responding to the other fictional characters or describing her own thoughts. Betty Draper's tweets (Betty is Don's frustrated wife, who ultimately ends up divorcing Don), written by Helen Klein Ross, are never out of character as "Ross can't help but expose Betty's feelings online in ways the character is never allowed to on the show" (Rose, page 81). This is shown, for example, when she tweets: "Eating lunch in the dining room. Housekeeper doing same in the kitchen. This feels odd. But it's not as if I could ask her to join me".

27

All this adds an extra layer to the character that would be hard to express through simple TV narration.

Not long after they started tweeting, both Don Draper's and Peggy Olson's accounts were suspended following AMC's request. This generated such an outburst in the online community that AMC finally allowed for the accounts to be put back up on Twitter, once the cable company realized that it was actually counterproductive to interrupt what effectively was free advertisement for the show.

The fact that people would want to tweet as their favorite show's characters shouldn't be too surprising. It is a reflection of what people expect from TV: as Frank Rose (2011) writes, "people want to be immersed. They want to get involved in a story, to carve out a role for themselves, to make it their own" (page 8). Interestingly, one of the aspects of this new media trend is that a social network like Twitter is allowing for the internal story-world of a TV show to extend into our own world, allowing viewers to fully bring fictional characters into their own lives. This also fundamentally proves that the lean-back experience that television has offered in the past is not necessarily what viewers expect to get from the medium. Rose (2011) argues that "the couch potato era [...] turns out to be less an era than a blip - and a blip based on faulty assumptions at that". Perhaps in the past it was simply the state of technology that didn't allow for the medium television to be fully exploited and to satisfy the viewers' true aspirations for sociality and interactivity. Furthermore, it seems that a new role for the user is emerging, a role which goes beyond that of consumer of content, as it was the case for 20th century mass media.

According to Rose (2011), the web is fostering the surfacing of a new type of narrative, "one that's told through many media at once in a way that's nonlinear, that's participatory and often game-like, and that's designed above all to be immersive. This is "deep media":stories that are not just entertaining but immersive, taking you deeper than an hour-long TV drama or a two-hour movie or a 30-second spot will permit" (page 3). This is obviously transforming both entertainment and advertising, which is also increasingly relying on the same techniques to offer better experiences to potential customers.

A TV show that took full advantage of the power of the Web is *Lost*, a complicated tale about a group of people who got stuck in an island following a plane crash. The show, which run from 2004 to 2010, told such a complicated story that the public was forced to get help from others online. A wiki dedicated to the show emerged as an autonomous effort of Kevin Croy, one of the many *Lost*'s fans. As of April 2011, *Lostpedia* has 7,202 articles dedicated to the TV show, its characters and its plot.

But not all of the "internet experience" came directly from the show's fan base. The show creators developed *The Lost Experience*, an alternative reality game, which played out in the U.S. in the break between the second and third season and in the U.K. during the second season. During the commercial breaks, Lost started airing commercials of the Hanso Foundation, which is a fictitious corporation frequently mentioned in the show. These commercials directed people to websites which were part of the *Lost Experience*. These websites would offer viewers extra information about the story and gave the public new material to develop new theories about what had happened in the island. Some of these websites were tied to specific sponsors of the show, allowing the producers to obtain extra income from the show. For example, one of the video which was part of the experience was hidden in a Jeep Compass product presentation page. Amongst the brands which took advantage of the experience, letting users find clues about the show while playing on their website or watching their commercials, there were Sprite, Monster.com and Verizon.

As Rose (2011) explains, "*Lost* relied for its effect on the hoarding and selective release of information. Occasionally the show's creators would part the curtain, giving the fans a tantalizing glimpse of something that would keep them occupied for months, if not years" (Page 166). This experience, which wouldn't have been equally compelling without the use of web tools, was instrumental in creating a passionate fan base, while also increasing *Lost*'s audience. It seems clear that as content creators produce shows in this era, they will have to think more and more about how to make the story as immersive as possible. The web will be fundamental to create such stories and experiences. Producers have also understood that a committed fan base can be a primary source of income for the show. In this era of viewership fragmentation, few "hardcore" fans can be sufficient to keep a show profitable (for example through the sale of show-related merchandise, DVDs, etc.).

On another note, a more flexible narrative has another very important consequence for today's society: while a dominant culture might still prevail, the definition of a common culture is in the hands of more people, who are now able to participate to the shaping of society by discussing online, sometimes even "imposing" their will from the bottom. For example, two characters from the show *Lost* were killed off from the show because viewers were complaining online that the two characters only turned up in the third season of the show and were simply too annoying. Other than for TV series as I argued above, this holds true, for example, for politics: politicians are nowadays almost immediately challenged if they provide viewers with false information during a television appearance. I believe that web-enabled ability of viewers to "talk back to the TV" is reducing the distance between Arnheim's "pathetic hermit" and the scene he experiences. In short, while this still happens, it has become harder for the most powerful to impose their ideas through television as TV has become a much less imposing medium. The more TV and web will converge into a unique entity, the more TV may become democratic.

3.3. Redefining Flow

As Thomson (2003) writes, flow "most basically means the scheduling of programs and the advertising breaks within and between them considered as a continuum" (page 6). Feuer (1983) explains how for Williams, who introduced the concept of flow, "the defining characteristic of broadcasting is one of sequence or flow. Thus the true series is not the published sequence of program items but this sequence transformed by another kind of sequence (advertising, previews, etc.)" (page 15). As social networks are becoming increasingly important in the television-watching experience, perhaps even the concept of flow should be reconsidered.

As television used to be more imposing on viewers, in a similar way the flow we experienced while watching "old television" was almost exclusively determined by the interests of networks and advertisers. What is happening now is that comments and conversations on social networks are increasingly becoming both elements of the flow and what actually define the flow itself. As mentioned above, with television and web converging into one element, it is impossible to separate what is said on social networks and the show itself, with social networks substantially becoming part of the flow itself. A recent report from Cisco (2011) gives a hint as to how social networks could define our programming flow: on the "10 Reasons You Won't Recognize Your Television in the Not-Too-Distant Future", the number one reason is the fact that channels will go away. With them, the experience of flow as a way channels and networks executives keep their viewers from one show to the other. More and more, it might not be a group of powerful producers that will define the sequence we watch. It is instead possible to imagine a flow defined by one's social network: whatever friends, acquaintances or the web talk about defines what we watch.

32

As Jenkins (2006) wrote, "Consumers are learning how to use these different media technologies to bring the flow of media more fully under their control and to interact with other consumers. The promises of this new media environment raise expectations of a freer flow of ideas and content. Inspired by those ideals, consumers are fighting for the right to participate more fully in their culture" (page 18).

4. YouTube and Internet videos

According to a survey from Nielsen (2011), people in the U.S. are watching always more videos online, so much as to threaten traditional television. While the number of online viewers only increased by 3 per cent in the last year, the time spent watching online video surged by 45 per cent, implying that those who consume online videos are increasingly watching entire shows online, as opposed to shorter videos.

4.1. YouTube

As more and more viewers rely on the web to find and watch TV shows and videos, several websites emerged to offer this service. The most popular website to watch online videos is certainly YouTube, one of the symbols of the web 2.0 era and one of its most popular websites and social networks. In few words, YouTube is a video sharing website where users can watch, upload and comment on videos.

YouTube ranks third according to Alexa (2011) amongst the most visited websites on the internet, right after Google and Facebook. According to comScore (2010), YouTube dominates the U.S market for online videos (a huge market considering that in May 2010, 183 million internet surfers watched online videos), with a market share of 43.1 %, a total of 14.6 billion videos viewed per month, with an average of more than 100 videos viewed per user. The website was launched in February 2005 and was bought by Google for $1.65 billion in November 2006.

Despite its relatively recent launch, YouTube already had a tremendous impact on society and it is increasingly shaping young people's cultural values. YouTube has launched music stars (for example Justin Bieber, a current teenagers' idol, was discovered by major studios because of the popularity of his YouTube channel), defined trends and promoted new forms of television and filmmaking.

On YouTube one can find user-generated content, TV clips, video clips, music videos, both at amateur level and at a professional one, uploaded by ordinary users, major studios, politicians, stars or even corporate brands. The majority of YouTube videos is so-called user generated content, but some of the major media corporations such as BBC, CBS, Vevo and Hulu also offer some of their original content as part of partnerships they have with YouTube.

According to the AFP (2010), by November 2010 YouTube had 35 hours of video uploaded per minute and by May 2010, it had more than 2 billion views per day (to give a sense of the website's growth, YouTube had announced on its website that it had reached 1 billion views per day in October 2009). According to Foley (2011), more content was uploaded on the website in two months than NBC, CBC and ABC broadcasted in 60 years.

Based on these facts, it cannot be ignored that YouTube occupies an important role in a discussion about television and its future as it is indeed contributing to the re-definition and re-shaping of the medium. What is probably the most interesting aspect of YouTube is that, as Strangelove (2010) suggests, "audiences are watching and interpreting YouTube videos not just as passive viewers but as active commentators and as producers of their own videos. The categories that once strictly divided society into producers and consumers are becoming increasingly blurred. The single social fact has significant implications for the next stage of capitalism and its media culture" (page 158).

What certainly is the most interesting aspect about YouTube is that it fosters ordinary citizen to express themselves, whether their ideas or their talents, and it allows these same ordinary citizens to find a public, even a very large one. This would have been impossible with "old-television" because people couldn't count on a convenient and cheap distribution system such as the internet.

YouTube's characteristics make it hard to define what YouTube really is. Is it TV? Is it another social network? Is it more simply a video aggregator? For example, in April 2010, YouTube started live-streaming the Indian Premiere League (IPL) games, further blurring the distinction between its offering and what is more commonly understood as television's offering. According to Sweney (2010), in a deal that reminds of television's contracts, YouTube obtained the rights to stream the matches for two years, while splitting the revenues from sponsorship and advertising with the IPL.

Furthermore, as already mentioned above, YouTube struck deals with several television and film producers. In November 2008, YouTube partnered with MGM Lions Gate Entertainment and CBS to let these companies upload full-length film and television shows in a special section of YouTube's website called "Shows". This was a major move against Hulu, a distant second in the online video market according to comCast (2010), but whose model is focused on showing professional TV content only (user generated videos are not allowed in the website). Hulu primarily features content from NBC, Fox and Disney (which are also joint owners of Hulu). In contrast to Hulu, which only operates in the U.S. market, YouTube has also launched a version of "Shows" for the British market in November 2009: according to Allen (2009), around 4000 full-length shows are offered from more than 60 partners.

YouTube offers partners the possibility to monetize their content by sharing advertising revenues with them. In particular, according to Google's corporate information, YouTube partners are entitled to a 68 % share of the earnings made from ads on the videos (Google/YouTube gets the remaining 32 %). Furthermore, YouTube allows partners to provide what YouTube's website describes as a "premium, lean-back viewing experience". In particular, "all videos are streamed at the highest possible quality—up to full 1080p HD if available—in a 16:9 aspect ratio player".

Another major advantage offered to YouTube's partners, which by now include ABC, CBS, Univision, Sony Pictures, Warner Brothers Pictures and Lionsgate, is that they are allowed to upload longer videos, with no length or size limit, avoiding the 15 minutes limit which is imposed to ordinary users. The result is that partners can have a "fully-branded channel", offering an experience which is not very different from that of "old-school TV", simply on a different screen.

Again, it seems hard to determine how YouTube stands in relation to television. What perhaps describe the phenomenon best is the concept of "convergence" between television and new media. According to Jenkins (2006), the era of media convergence is where "old and new media collide, where grassroots and corporate media intersect, where the power of the media producer and the power of the media consumer interact in unpredictable ways" (page 2).

Considering media convergence, YouTube can legitimately be thought of as a component of television, together with broadcast or cable channels . For example, shows such as "Dr. Horrible Sing Along Blog" and "The Guild", amongst others, are almost universally recognized as television despite the fact that they have never been neither on broadcast nor on cable TV. Dr. Horrible Sing Along Blog was developed during the writers' strike and was even awarded an Emmy award (again, without never being aired on standard television). The show was released online in three episodes of about fourteen minutes each and featured famous TV actors. Similarly, "The Guild" stars a famous TV actress, Felicia Day (who was also starring in Dr. Horrible), and premiered on YouTube on the 27th of July 2007. Subsequently it premiered on Microsoft's Xbox Live Marketplace, Zune Marketplace, and MSN Video. What makes these web series so obviously television may be the use of actors borrowed from traditional television, but more so the episodic structure of these experiments. Indeed Jenkins (2009) argues that "television may be a genre or format of entertainment - which looks and feels "like television" even if it is never broadcast. Here, television may refer to a form of storytelling which comes in short chunks which are organized as part of longer series which unfold across seasons."

YouTube's convergence to TV is also proven by the launch of "YouTube for TV" and later of "YouTube XL", a version of the website which has an interface designed to allow viewing of YouTube on the traditional television screen. On the content side, not only has YouTube partnered with several production companies, but in April 2011 the Wall Street Journal reported that YouTube "is planning to spend as much as $100 million to commission low-cost content designed exclusively for the Web" and it is looking to launch about 20 "premium channels" which would feature five to ten hours of professionally-produced original programming a week, in order to persuade users to spend more time on the website and convince advertisers that it can reach sought out consumers without doing any harm to their brands. Advertisers are in fact usually cautious to advertise next to user-generated content because they fear it might be of poor-quality or controversial.

4.1.1. YouTube and Society

The impact of YouTube on both internet culture and mainstream culture is evident and can be explained through several examples. One of the early examples is the case of "The Bus Uncle" Video. The video takes place on a bus in Hong Kong and shows a man screaming at a younger passenger who had asked him to be quieter on the phone. The event was secretly recorded with a cell phone by another passenger of the bus and quickly became a sensation on YouTube and was widely "discussed" on the mainstream media. While the video is not of the best quality, it had an outstanding diffusion and it became the most watched video on YouTube in May 2006, accumulating more than 3 million views in that month only (and it was only the beginning of YouTube). As it then became a tradition for the YouTube community, many "mocking versions" of the video were developed: as Bray (2006) reported, there were, amongst others, "the Karaoke version, the rap remix and the dance and disco take". Again, in line with what later became commonplace, the protagonists of the video were elevated to "celebrity status", with newspapers dedicating first pages to the event and the people involved.

What made this video so successful, which is probably one of the reasons YouTube itself became so successful is that it is perceived as a fair, unmediated representation of reality. As explained by Bray (2006), "*Bus Uncle* is seen as real, strong and honest, using language close to the heart of Hong Kong people and catching the collective emotional pulse in a city where people live cheek to jowl, and don't generally socialize with strangers or say how they feel". Perhaps it is this strong connection between YouTube and reality that made it so successful as it had been the case for television, whose style together with its association with liveness, made it perceived as more real than film.

While YouTube is increasingly offering the possibility to upload and watch professional TV-like content, YouTube's early success is indeed mainly due to the opportunity it gave to ordinary people to upload their videos, share them and eventually make them a success. In spite of video-sharing being one of the most common things to do on the web now, prior to YouTube's launch in 2005 there were very few easy and accessible websites for average computer users to post videos online. One of the effects of this on society is that it became much easier for an ordinary person, without excessive video-production means or capabilities, to reach a very wide and international audience. It could be said that there has been a democratization of the content production process.

Foley (2011) reports that 86 per cent of the 100 most-watched videos on YouTube is professionally made. Despite this, there still are many examples of extremely popular user generated videos. For example, "Charlie Bit My Finger" is the most watched of the user generated videos, having amassed a total of more than 300 million views as of May 2011. The clip is very simple, showing Charlie, one year old, biting the finger of his brother Harry, three years old, and then laughing about it while his older brother cries out: "Charly bit my finger...again!". The video was ranked first in Time's list of the "50 greatest viral videos of all time". While the comic-aspect and the realism of this family situation definitely facilitated the fame of the video, two other interesting aspects of YouTube emerge: first, the simplicity with which a video can go viral and second, the massive amount of viewers for such a video, a number which is much higher than any TV show could expect. This last aspect highlights one other characteristic of YouTube, which is the fact that it operates on a much bigger market and serves many more people than a traditional TV channel. Furthermore, YouTube appears to have a much broader international reach than whatever American network might have and might therefore have a much more significant impact on today's global culture.

4.2. Beyond YouTube

While YouTube is certainly the most successful of the web applications to watch videos, there are other successful examples. Hulu, as mentioned above, focusing on TV shows, offers an experience much more similar to that of traditional TV, with exclusively professional content and a much higher frequency of commercials "interrupting" the viewing experience. Furthermore, the networks themselves, once understood that the internet phenomena was not going to end any time soon, developed the websites of their own shows, often offering the latest clips from the shows and in many instances (such as for "Modern Family" and "How I met your Mother, amongst many others) the complete streaming of the latest few episodes aired.

The more time it passes, the more it becomes clear that watching TV on the internet and browsing the internet on television will become more and more common place, as web and TV converge into a unique experience and a unique device for their consumption is developed. For example Google, which already owns YouTube, has developed "Google TV", its own way to bring the internet on the television set. With Google TV, users can watch TV and browse the internet using Google's internet browser Chrome. Google's search function facilitates the search of TV content. As reported by the New York Times (2010), "Google promises to apply its main expertise — search — to the TV. Instead of the byzantine cable and DVR programming menus that viewers navigate today, with Google TV, they can search for the name of a show and see when it's being broadcast and where it's available online, in addition to viewing links to Web sites about the show and its actors."

Google TV also offers several apps for television (such as Netflix, Pandora, Amazon, Napster and Twitter) and developers will soon be able to create and sell their own TV apps through the Android store. Furthermore, users are able to tweet about their show on the same screen where they watch the show.
The technology has proven of good quality, with computer-like capabilities. However, according to the New York Times (2011) and several other reviewers, the product is for the moment disappointing. As Kevin Sintumuang (2010) wrote on the Wall Street Journal, "the potential is as big as, well, the internet, but right now Google TV is a bit of a tease".

What seems to be the problem is that, while people can watch TV shows and movies using Netflix or Amazon on the Google TV platform (provided that they pay Netflix's or Amazon's subscription fee), and they can also watch the regular programming, the major networks (such as NBC, CBS, ABC and even Hulu) are not allowing viewers to watch the full-length shows that they offer on their websites on Google TV. To be fair, this is a not a particularly surprising behavior since it seems to represent the typical industry reaction when anything new and potentially disruptive comes out. This was the case with the VCR (which ultimately turned into a very remunerative business opportunity), the DVR and the internet in general. In order for Google TV to be a success, both parties

(Google and TV content producers) will have to figure out a strategy to leverage each other's strengths. For the moment, Google's answer to distrustful networks seems to be the recently announced $100 million investment in the production of YouTube content. But I believe that in an era in which immersion in the story and interactivity are fundamental to create successful TV shows, content creators could take advantage of Google TV inherent interactivity to offer the public the best possible experience. In fact, while many people already use several devices at once, by allowing people to more easily tweet, comment and get external information while watching a TV show, Google TV could really represent a boost to the interactivity of television programs. Also from an advertising perspective, Google TV could offer the networks much better targeted advertising, thanks to the search information it retains, consequently augmenting the Cost-per-Thousand-Impressions (CPM) that advertisers would be willing to pay for an ad to appear during a TV show. With improving technologies, advertisers might also be able to offer viewers the possibility to, for example, click on one of the show's characters to find out what he/she is wearing and then offer different options as to where to buy the product.

However one feels about watching TV on the internet or surfing the internet on television, it is by now clear that this trend is exploding and it's going to play a fundamental role in the future of television.

5. The Future of Television in 10 trends

"Future TV may be unrecognizable from today, defined not just by linear TV channels, packaged and scheduled by television executives, but instead it will resemble more of a kaleidoscope, thousands of streams of content, some indistinguishable as actual channels. These streams will mix together broadcasters' content and programs, and our viewer's contributions. At the simplest level – audiences will want to organize and reorganize content the way they want it. They'll add comments to our programs, vote on them, and generally mess about with them. But on another level, audiences will want to create these streams of video themselves from scratch, with or without our help. At this end of the spectrum, the traditional "monologue broadcaster" to "grateful viewer" relationship will break down". This is a statement that Ashley Highfield, director of BBC New Media and Technology, made in October 2003, proving how industry experts have sometimes been extremely insightful in predicting what the future of TV was going to be.

As television has changed a lot in the past few years, it is reasonable to believe that it will keep on changing in the future, most probably at an even faster rate. The Cisco Internet Business Solutions Group (IBSG) recently wrote a very interesting study on the "10 Reasons You Won't Recognize Your Television in the Not-Too-Distant Future". Cisco interviewed more than 50 television experts (producers, engineers and academics) to get a sense of what TV will be like in the not-too-distant future. While the experts had to express their opinions relative to what TV will be in 20 years from now, some of their predictions might materialize much earlier than that. From my summary of the report, it will become apparent that the general consensus is that television will be revolutionized, again.

The report nicely structures some of the issues already covered in this thesis, such as the users' new relation to content production and the fact that TV will be watched on multiple devices, but it also adds some interesting technological forecasts, such as the eventual introduction of olfactory elements and tactile reproduction to the TV experience. Some of the trends mentioned in the report are already partially reality. In the future they will become more common.

Through most of these ten predictions, listed below, it is apparent that television will become always more social.

5.1. Channels will go away

According to the experts interviewed, "most viewers will watch customized, on-demand streams, or they will access unlimited content from available libraries using powerful search/recommendation engines" (page 2). Indeed the number of channels is so high that it has become extremely cumbersome for viewers to find the content that would best fulfill their interests. With the certain diffusion of internet-connected television, thanks to devices such as Google TV, but also, amongst others, Roku, Boxee and Apple TV, consumer will be discovering content as they do on the internet, through search engines, reducing the importance of channels, which have in fact become less and less of a coherent agglomerate of content and act more and more as VC-like investors, financing the shows that they believe will be most profitable.

5.2. Kiss the remote goodbye

According to the experts interviewed, "consumers will use natural language, gestures, and adjunct devices such as smartphones and iPads to interact with their TVs as easily as they do with another person" (page 2). Boxee already allows users to use the iPhone as remote control, and several other companies, such as Verizon and Comcast, are offering their costumers the possibility to control the TV using their smartphones.

5.3. Screens Do Anything, Anywhere

According to CISCO's report, in twenty years Americans won't be investing in buying televisions, but they will buy screens: "Some will be thinner, larger, and have even higher definition than the ones we know today. Some could occupy a whole wall. Many will be contained within the higher-quality descendents of the portable devices we carry in our pockets today, such as smartphones, tablet PCs, and portable gaming players. Some may be expandable, flexible, or even wearable. Screens will be everywhere, and each screen will be multipurpose" (page 3). According to the experts, the television experience will be detached from a specific device as most devices will be multifunctional. In particular smartphones might play a very important role in television's future, especially as internet connection on mobile phones becomes always faster, allowing for videos to be watched without continuous interruptions.

5.4. Ads get personal

According to the report, in 20 years, "the majority of ads will be contextual, highly interactive, and laser-targeted to each viewer" (page 4) and viewers will be pointing or clicking on whatever object featured in a television show to receive advertising information. For example, when pointing at the BMW in the latest James Bond movie, one could be given information about the models available.

5.5. Don't Just Watch—Get Involved

As already mentioned before, nowadays most content needs to be interactive and immersive to attract a loyal group of followers. Interaction for now happens mainly through gaming, social media and the shows' websites. This trend is destined to become always more important in the future 20 years. For example, "viewers may "friend" their favorite TV characters or investigate plot twists using resources in their own communities" (page 4).

5.6. Watch Together, Virtually

Watching TV with family members or friends has always been part of the television experience. As people can communicate always more easily, it will become commonplace to invite friends and family to watch TV together in virtual settings, even when staying in opposite parts of the world.

5.7. Is It Real, or Is It Television?

According to CISCO's survey, "advances in the TV-viewing experience will introduce new sensory elements and enable consumers to have more choice in how they interact with their content" (page 5). For example, olfactory elements and the possibility of tactile reproduction will be offered, just as sound is offered today.

5.8. Your TV Follows You

According to the experts interviewed, TV content will be accessible anywhere at whatever time. People will be able to able to watch TV when in line at the supermarket, on the bus, fundamentally everywhere. For example, apps such as Netflix and Hulu are already available for smartphones.

5.9. "Regular Joes" Go Hollywood

The trend that has seen more and more amateur film and TV-making will continue and new methods to finance, create and deliver content to the masses will flourish. At the same time, as tools to edit and produce content become always cheaper and easier to use, the user-generated content will strongly increase in quality. Viral marketing, which is easier to implement thanks to social networks, will allow independent producers to easily promote their work. The result will be a very long tail of content, with user-generated videos served side by side to the professional studio content.

5.10. Creation Goes Viral

Even the way the narration is unfolded and scripts are created might change. Content creators will most probably invite the public to participate in the creation process. For example, people might be able to participate in online collaboration sessions to develop new ideas for the next episode of a show, up to few days prior to the airing of the episode. Should this become commonplace, obviously production rules would have to change, with filming of episodes done in a much more limited amount of time.

6. Conclusion

It is by now impossible not to acknowledge the potential that television has not only as a mere influence on society, but also as a driving force for social interaction. In particular, I have shown how the World Wide Web and social networks such as Twitter and Facebook have made the television experience much more interactive and social than it used to be. Not only they have proved that television's true nature is a social one and that the couch potato era was just a "blip based on faulty assumptions", but they fostered the rediscovery of what are considered the most fundamental properties of television. Indeed, I have shown how social networks re-imposed liveness on the audience as a condition to participate in the collective conversation that has become integrating part of the TV experience. Social networks have also extended the importance of character-centric storylines by bringing fictitious characters into people's lives as it was the case of *Mad Men*'s fans who started twitting as their favorite characters. Finally, even flow has been refined by social networks, which are now increasingly taking the role of the broadcasting networks and cable channels in determining what we watch. What appears to be the axiomatic, defining characteristic of television is therefore its social essence, which functions as a glue that keeps together all of its other characteristics.

Furthermore, television is increasingly detaching itself from its connection to the black box that we have traditionally associated with TV. In the chapter about YouTube, I have argued that the content watched might be more important than the device on which it is watched to determine whether one is watching TV. This consideration is particularly important since the web seems to have increasingly become the place where viewers get their content and since a whole new range of devices is increasingly used to consume content, from tablets such as the iPad to mobile phones, which are quickly becoming one of the main tools that people use to watch their favorite videos and shows.

It is by now obvious that television has been completely revolutionized by the internet. With the continuous convergence of television and web, it nowadays seems impossible to venture a univocal definition for television. What might be the solution, as Nicholas Negroponte (chairman emeritus of the MIT Media Lab) said, is "to stop thinking of television as television". It doesn't matter where one watches TV anymore, whether it is on a black box, on a computer screen or even on a mobile phone. It still is television.

What is certain is that television has become a more participative medium. We are quickly abandoning the traditional paradigm that has long seen television as an "imposing medium", something that could allow few people in charge to define trends and opinions without any mediation from the viewers. On the one hand, today's viewers are also producers and on the other hand, today's viewers can use the web to respond, comment and critique to anything they watch on TV. This is why television producers have slowly started to recognize the importance of involving the public by asking viewers to participate in online games and riddles or by making more complex stories that require a truly engaged audience.

Despite all the changes, television is certainly not dying. It is far from dead. Jenkins (2006) explains it best: "a medium's content may shift [...], its audience may change [...], and its social status may raise or fall [...], but once a medium establishes itself as satisfying some core human demand, it continues to function within the larger system of communications options" (page 14). In particular, television has certainly changed definition and its definition will keep on changing in the future. Whether one trusts or not the judgment of the experts interviewed by CISCO, it is clear that television will keep on changing and even few years from now it will offer a completely different experience from the one it offers today. I cannot help but being relieved that, however television will look like in the future, we will all be able to contribute extensively to its improvement, while the TV experience will also be always more entertaining for each one of us.

7. References

AFP . (2010, November 11). 35 hours of video a minute uploaded to YouTube. Retrieved from http://www.google.com/hostednews/afp/article/ALeqM5hL4UMqXBKBTfJ2PjHI NPGpWZe82w?docId=CNG.7a039cc7305a51102e864beb3aa51545.181

Allen, E.T. *The Kennedy-Nixon Presidential Debates, 1960.* Retrieved from http://www.museum.tv/eotvsection.php?entrycode=kennedy-nixon

Allen, K. (2009, November 19). YouTube launches UK TV section with more than 60 partners. *The Guardian.* Retrieved from http://www.guardian.co.uk/media/2009/nov/19/youtube-uk-full-length-shows

Arnheim, R. (1935). *A Forecast of Television*. Berkeley, CA: University of California Press

Bauder, D. (2010, August 17). Survey shows extent of TV time shifting. *Associated Press.* Retrieved from http://today.msnbc.msn.com/id/38737094/ns/today-entertainment/from/toolbar

Bray, M. (2006, June 9). Irate HK man unlikely Web hero. *CNN International.* Retrieved from http://edition.cnn.com/2006/WORLD/asiapcf/06/07/hk.uncle/

*comScore. (*2010, June 24). comScore Releases May 2010 U.S. Online Video Rankings. Retrieved from http://www.comscore.com/Press_Events/Press_Releases/2010/6/comScore_R eleases_May_2010_U.S._Online_Video_Rankings

Cordero, C., Gerhardt, W., Griffin, K., Izdebski, L., Parsons, D. & Puopolo, S. (2011). *The Future of Television: Sweeping Change at B reakneck Speed.* San Jose, CA: Cisco

Craig, E. (2010, November 5). 10 Reasons Every TV Exec Needs to Start Tweeting. *Mashable.* Retrieved from http://mashable.com/2010/11/05/tv-executives-twitter/?utm_source=feedburner&utm_medium=feed&utm_campaign=Feed:+Mashable+%28Mashable%29

The Economist. (2010, April 29). *The lazy medium - How people really watch television.* Retrieved from (I should mention the whole report on TV)http://www.economist.com/node/15980817?story_id=15980817

Feuer, J. (1983). *The concept of Live Television: Ontology as Ideology.* Los Angeles, CA: The American Film Institute

Fletcher, D. (2010, March 29). YouTube's 50 Best Videos. *Time.* Retrieved from http://www.time.com/time/specials/packages/article/0,28804,1974961_19749 25,00.html

Foley, S. (2011, March 29). YouTube takes on television with star cast. *The Independent.* Retrieved from http://www.independent.co.uk/arts-entertainment/tv/news/youtube-takes-on-television-with-star-cast-2255762.html

Gitelman, L. (2008, September 30). *Always Already New: Media, History, and the Data of Culture*. Cambridge, MA: The MIT Press.

Harboe, G., Massey, N., Metcalf, C., Wheatley, D. & Romano, G. (2008). *The uses of social television*. Schaumburg, IL: Motorola

International Television Expert Group. (April 2010). World Television Market (2008-2013). *Itve.org.* Retrieved from http://www.international-television.org/tv_market_data/world-tv-market-2010.html

Jenkins, H. (2009, September 29). In a Social Networking world, what's the future of TV? *Huffington Post.* Retrieved from http://www.huffingtonpost.com/henry-jenkins/in-a-social-networking-wo_b_292014.html

Jenkins, H. (2006, August 1). *Convergence Culture: Where Old and New Media Collide.* New York, NY: NYU Press

Klym, N. & Montpetit, M. (2008, September 1). *Innovation at the Edge: Social TV and Beyond.* Cambridge, MA: MIT Communications Futures Program (CFP).

Kramer, C. (2011). *mobilebehavior.com.* Retrieved from http://www.slideshare.net/tribaldb/hybrid-media-how-social-is-enabling-event-tv

Lotz Amanda. (2007). *The Television will be revolutionized.* New York, NY: New York University Press

McGirt, E. (2010, November 22). I want my Twitter TV. *Fast Company.* Retrieved from http://www.fastcompany.com/magazine/151/i-want-my-twitter-tv.html

Melanson, M. – Jan 19 2011. What Glee Means for Twitter & Television. *Read Write Web.* Retrieved from http://www.readwriteweb.com/archives/what_glee_means_for_twitter_television.php

Miller, C. & Vance, A. (2010, December 19). Google TV Faces Delays Amid Poor Reviews. *New York Times.* Retrieved from http://www.nytimes.com/2010/12/20/technology/20google.html

Mittell, J. (2003, May 3). *Interfacing Television: TiVo, Technological Convergence, and Everyday Life.* Cambridge, MA: MIT3 Conference

Nielsen report data retrieved from

http://www.marketingcharts.com/television/timeshifted-tv-viewing-up-13-yoy-in-q4-10-16563/nielsen-q4tv-time-spent-monthly-mar-2011jpg/

Poniewozik, J. (2010, March 22). Twitter and TV: How Social Media Is Helping Old Media". *Time.* Retrieved from http://www.time.com/time/magazine/article/0,9171,1971444,00.html

Rose, F. (2011). *The art of Immersion.* New York, NY: W.W. Norton & Company, Inc.

Ryan, M-L. (2006). *Avatars of Story.* Minneapolis, MN: University of Minnesota Press

Silverman, M. (2011, February 19). Top 10 Twitter Trends This Week [CHART]. *Mashable.* Retrieved from http://mashable.com/2011/02/19/trending-topics-chart-twitter/

Silverman, M. (2010, December 22). What Twitter's Trending Topics Told Us About the World in 2010 [CHARTS]. *Mashable.* Retrieved from http://mashable.com/2010/12/22/top-twitter-trends-2010-charts/

Sintumuang, K. (2010, November 13). Testing Google TV: How'd This LOLCat Get on My Flat-Screen. *The Wall Street Journal.* Retrieved from http://online.wsj.com/article/SB100014240527487046357045756045226576009254.html

Stelter, B. (2011, February 20). TV Industry Taps Social Media to Keep Viewers' Attention. *The New York Times.* Retrieved from http://www.nytimes.com/2011/02/21/business/media/21watercooler.html?pagewanted=1&_r=1

Sterling, B. (1995). The Dead Media Manifesto. Retrieved from http://www.alamut.com/subj/artiface/deadMedia/dM_Manifesto.html

Strangelove, M. (April 30, 2010). *Watching YouTube: Extraordinary Videos by Ordinary People.* Toronto, Canada: University of Toronto Press, Scholarly Publishing Division

Sweney, M. (2010, January 20). YouTube confirms worldwide deal for live Indian Premier League cricket. *The Guardian.* Retrieved from

http://www.guardian.co.uk/media/2010/jan/20/youtube-live-indian-premier-league

Thompson, K. (2003). *Storytelling in Film and Television.* Cambridge, MA: Harvard University Press

Tsotsis, A. (2011, February 28). The Oscars, On Twitter: Over 1.2 Million Tweets, 388K Users Tweeting. *Techcrunch.* Retrieved from

http://techcrunch.com/2011/02/28/the-oscars-twitter/

Williams, R. (1974). *Television.* London, UK: Fontana

Yong, K. (2009, June 2). Experience YouTube XL on the Big Screen. *YouTube Blog.* Retrieved from

http://youtube-global.blogspot.com/2009/06/experience-youtube-xl-on-big-screen_02.html

YouTube Website. http://www.youtube.com